Embracing Growth

A Journey of Self-Exploration and Transformation

Written By

Dr. Jesse Sanders, Ph.D.

Introduction

Welcome to "Embracing Growth: A Journey of Self-Exploration and Transformation." This eBook is a guide to navigating the complexities of personal development and cultivating a life filled with meaning, purpose, and fulfillment. In these pages, you will embark on a journey of self-discovery, healing, and growth, exploring the depths of your being and unlocking your true potential.

Life is a journey of constant evolution and change, and each of us holds within us the power to shape our own destiny. Yet, the path to personal growth is often filled with obstacles, challenges, and moments of uncertainty. It requires courage, self- awareness, and a willingness to confront the parts of ourselves that may be holding us back.

In this eBook, we will delve into the fundamental principles of personal growth and transformation, offering insights, strategies, and practical tools to help you navigate the complexities of the human experience. From cultivating self-love and acceptance to healing past wounds and embracing change, each chapter is designed to guide you on your quest towards a more authentic, purposeful, and fulfilling life.

Throughout this journey, you will learn to embrace vulnerability, cultivate resilience, and harness the power of self-discovery to create positive change in your life and the lives of those around you. You will explore the importance of self-care, mindfulness, and self-compassion as essential pillars of personal well- being and inner peace.

As you embark on this journey of self-exploration and transformation, remember that you are not alone. You are part of a community of individuals who are committed to growth, healing, and living their best lives. Together, we can support and uplift each other as we navigate the ups and downs of the human experience. So, I invite you to embark on this journey with an open heart and an open mind.

Embrace the challenges, celebrate the victories, and trust in the wisdom of your own inner voice. May this eBook serve as a guiding light on your path towards greater self-awareness, fulfillment, and joy.

Here's to embracing growth and transforming our lives from the inside out.

The Examination

Examining, healing, and implementing change within ourselves and those around us is a multifaceted process that requires self-awareness, compassion, and dedication. Here are some steps to begin this journey:

- **Self-Reflection:** Start by engaging in introspection and self- reflection to gain insight into your thoughts, feelings, and behaviors. Consider journaling, meditation, or therapy as tools for exploring your inner landscape and understanding the patterns that may be influencing your life.

- **Identify Areas for Growth:** Take stock of areas in your life where you would like to see improvement or change. This could include relationships, career goals, personal habits, or emotional well-being. Be honest with yourself about areas where you may be struggling or feeling stuck.

- **Set Intentions:** Clarify your intentions for personal growth and transformation. What do you hope to achieve? What values do you want to embody?

Setting clear intentions can help guide your actions and decisions as you move forward.

- **Practice Self-Compassion:** Cultivate self-compassion as you navigate the process of change. Be kind and understanding towards yourself, especially when facing challenges or setbacks. Treat yourself with the same kindness and empathy that you would offer to a friend in need.

- **Seek Support:** Reach out to trusted friends, family members, mentors, or therapists for support and guidance. Surround yourself with people who uplift and encourage you on your journey towards growth and healing.

- **Embrace Vulnerability:** Allow yourself to be vulnerable and open to the process of transformation. Recognize that growth often involves discomfort and uncertainty, but it also offers opportunities for learning and expansion.

- **Practice Mindfulness:** Cultivate mindfulness practices to bring awareness to the present moment and observe your thoughts, emotions, and sensations without judgment. Mindfulness can help you develop greater clarity, resilience, and inner peace amidst life's challenges.

- **Take Action:** Take concrete steps towards implementing change in your life. This may involve setting goals, creating action plans, and taking consistent, intentional steps towards your desired outcomes.

- **Be Patient and Persistent:** Understand that personal growth is a journey that unfolds over time. Be patient with yourself and trust in the process, even when progress feels slow or uncertain. Stay committed to your goals and keep moving forward with determination.

- **Lead by Example:** Model the change you wish to see in the world by embodying your values and principles in your actions and interactions with others. Inspire and empower those around you to embark on their own journey of self-exploration and growth.

By engaging in this process of self-examination, healing, and implementation of change, you can cultivate greater self-awareness, resilience, and fulfillment in your own life, while also positively impacting those around you. Remember that personal growth is an ongoing journey, and every step you take towards self- improvement brings you closer to living a more authentic and meaningful life.

There are two important definitions that are imperative during this Redefining journey, and they are: redefined, which is to reexamine or reevaluate especially with a view to change. The second word is health, which is the condition of being sound in body, mind, or spirit: a condition in which someone or something is thriving or doing well.

The beginning of acknowledgement and healing is dealing/confronting with the pain (acute mental or emotional distress or suffering; trouble, care, or effort taken to accomplish something)

- ▶ Dysfunction or pain can start with one person and begin to manifest/transfer to all of those that are connected.
- ▶ The family should be an interacting unit that strives to achieve balance in relationships through the use of repetitious, circular, and predictable communication patterns. (Everyone should know what's important, the communication, and the direction)
- ▶ It is difficult for a family unit to become strong and redefined if one or multiple people suffer from low esteem. A person that has low self-esteem deals with a great sense of anxiety and uncertainty about themselves. Therefore, they do not exercise stability within themselves or the unit.
- ▶ As individuals suffering from low self-esteem feel they have nothing to offer and should not be expected to give anything.

The Call to Adventure

You are being introduced to the concept of the call to adventure—a pivotal moment in your life when you feel a deep sense of longing for growth and self-realization.

This reading serves as a catalyst for you to recognize and embrace the opportunities for personal growth that lies ahead.

As we stand at the threshold of endless possibilities, I invite you to reflect on your aspirations, dreams, and deepest desires. Emphasizing the importance of courage, resilience, and a willingness to embrace change as essential qualities for embarking on the journey of self-exploration and transformation.

Through relatable anecdotes, inspirational quotes, and thought-provoking questions, you can become encouraged to consider the ways in which you have already answered the call to adventure in your own life. Inviting you to reflect on past experiences of growth and transformation, as well as moments of fear, uncertainty, and doubt that may have held you back.

Let's set the stage for the transformative journey that lies ahead, while being challenged to step out of your comfort zones and into the unknown. Be encouraged to embrace the inherent risks and rewards of growth, trusting in your ability to navigate the challenges and opportunities that awaits you.

Navigating Inner Waters

Now let us delve into the process of navigating inner waters—a metaphor for exploring the depths of our being. This section invites you to embark on a journey of introspection and self-examination, diving deep into the core of your identity and consciousness.

Exploring the depths of our inner world can be both exhilarating and challenging. Just as the vast expanse of the ocean holds mysteries waiting to be discovered, so too does our inner landscape contain hidden truths about ourselves. Through introspection, reflection, and self-examination, you are encouraged to uncover these truths, shedding light on your strengths, weaknesses, fears, and aspirations.

There is a fundamental importance of self-awareness as a foundation for personal growth and transformation. By gaining insight into our thoughts, emotions, and behaviors, we become better equipped to navigate the complexities of life and make conscious choices aligned with our values and aspirations.

Through a series of guided exercises, journal prompts, and reflective practices, you are invited to explore various aspects of your inner world, including your beliefs, values, desires, fears, and dreams. You are encouraged to confront limiting beliefs, overcome inner obstacles, and cultivate a deeper sense of self-compassion and acceptance.

Navigating inner waters requires courage, vulnerability, and a willingness to confront discomfort and uncertainty. However, it is through this process of self- exploration that you can tap into your inner wisdom, resilience, and authenticity, ultimately empowering you to lead more fulfilling and meaningful life.

This serves as a reminder that the journey of self-exploration is ongoing and dynamic, requiring patience, curiosity, and an open heart. By navigating inner waters with courage and self-compassion, you can uncover your true essence and embrace the transformative power of personal growth and self-discovery.

Cultivating Resilience

We will now explore the theme of cultivating resilience in the face of life's challenges. Emphasizing that while adversity and setbacks are inevitable parts of the human experience, our response to them plays a crucial role in shaping our growth and development.

Life's challenges can take many forms whether it be loss, failure, rejection, or unexpected change. However, it is not the challenges themselves but rather our response to them that determines our ability to thrive in the face of adversity.

Cultivating resilience involves developing the inner strength, adaptability, and resourcefulness to navigate obstacles with grace and determination.

You are encouraged to adopt a growth mindset an attitude that views challenges as opportunities for learning and growth rather than insurmountable barriers. By reframing setbacks as valuable lessons and opportunities for personal development, individuals can cultivate resilience and bounce back stronger than before.

You are being offered practical strategies and exercises for building resilience, including:

- **Developing self-awareness:** By understanding our thoughts, emotions, and patterns of behavior, we can better navigate difficult situations and manage stress more effectively.

- **Cultivating self-compassion:** Treating ourselves with kindness and compassion in times of struggle allows us to bounce back from setbacks with greater resilience and confidence.

- **Building a support network:** Surrounding ourselves with supportive relationships and seeking help when needed can provide invaluable emotional support and encouragement during challenging times.

- **Practicing mindfulness:** Mindfulness practices such as meditation, deep breathing, and yoga can help cultivate resilience by promoting relaxation, stress reduction, and emotional regulation.

- **Finding meaning and purpose:** Connecting with our values, passions, and sense of purpose can provide a sense of meaning and direction, even in the face of adversity.

Ultimately, cultivating resilience is a journey of self-discovery and growth—one that requires patience, perseverance, and self-compassion. By embracing life's challenges as opportunities for growth and learning, individuals can cultivate resilience and emerge stronger, wiser, and more resilient than before.

Unleashing Potential

Let us now delve into the theme of unleashing potential—a concept centered around the idea that everyone possesses unique talents, strengths, and capabilities waiting to be discovered and actualized.

We will begin by emphasizing the importance of setting clear goals and intentions as a foundational step toward unleashing one's potential. By identifying what we truly desire and envisioning our ideal future, we can create a roadmap for personal and professional growth. Setting specific, measurable, achievable, relevant, and time- bound (SMART) goals provides a framework for progress and allows us to track our development over time.

Additionally, cultivating a growth mindset is highlighted as essential for unlocking potential. A growth mindset is characterized by a belief in the power of effort, learning, and resilience to fuel personal growth and success. By adopting a mindset that views challenges as opportunities for growth and setbacks as valuable learning experiences, individuals can overcome self-limiting beliefs and tap into their full potential.

Taking consistent action toward our goals is emphasized as a key component of unleashing potential. By breaking goals down into manageable steps and taking intentional action each day, we can gradually move closer to our aspirations and create momentum toward our desired outcomes. Consistency, discipline, and perseverance are essential qualities for sustained growth and achievement.

This section offers practical strategies and exercises for unleashing potential, including:

- **Self-reflection and self-awareness:** Identifying our strengths, values, and passions allows us to align our goals with our authentic selves and leverage our unique talents and abilities.
- **Building confidence and self-efficacy:** Cultivating belief in our ability to overcome obstacles and achieve our goals empowers us to take bold action and pursue our dreams with courage and conviction.

- **Seeking feedback and support:** Soliciting input from mentors, coaches, and peers can provide valuable insights and guidance for personal and professional development.
- **Embracing challenges and growth opportunities:** Stepping outside our comfort zones, embracing uncertainty, and tackling new challenges fosters resilience, adaptability, and growth.
- **Celebrating progress and milestones:** Acknowledging and celebrating our achievements along the way reinforces positive habits, boosts motivation, and sustains momentum toward our goals.

Ultimately, unleashing potential is a transformative journey of self-discovery, growth, and empowerment—one that requires courage, commitment, and a willingness to embrace change. By setting bold goals, cultivating a growth mindset, and taking consistent action, individuals can unlock their true potential and create a life of purpose, passion, and fulfillment.

Embracing Change

In Embracing Growth, we are now going to explore the theme of embracing change—a fundamental aspect of the human experience that is both inevitable and transformative.

We will begin by acknowledging the universal truth that change is the only constant in life. From the natural cycles of growth and decay to the unpredictable twists and turns of our personal journeys, change permeates every aspect of our existence.

However, despite its inevitability, many individuals struggle to embrace change due to fear of the unknown, uncertainty, and discomfort associated with stepping outside of their comfort zones.

Embracing change involves cultivating a mindset of openness, adaptability, and resilience in the face of life's inevitable transitions. It requires a willingness to let go of outdated beliefs, patterns, and behaviors that no longer serve us and embrace new opportunities for growth and transformation.

One of the key principles of embracing change is recognizing that every challenge, setback, and transition presents an opportunity for learning and personal development. By reframing change as a catalyst for growth rather than a threat to stability, individuals can approach life's transitions with curiosity, optimism, and a sense of adventure.

This section explores various strategies and practices for embracing change, including:

- **Cultivating mindfulness and presence:** By practicing mindfulness and staying present in the moment, individuals can develop greater awareness of their thoughts, emotions, and reactions to change. Mindfulness helps cultivate a sense of inner calm and resilience, enabling individuals to navigate transitions with greater clarity and equanimity.

- **Adopting a growth mindset:** Embracing change requires viewing challenges as opportunities for growth and learning. A growth mindset is characterized by a belief in one's capacity to learn, adapt, and grow in response to adversity. By reframing setbacks as valuable learning experiences, individuals can approach change with a sense of curiosity and optimism.

- **Building resilience:** Resilience is the ability to bounce back from adversity and adapt to changing circumstances. By developing resilience through practices such as self-care, social support, and positive coping strategies, individuals can better navigate life's ups and downs with grace and fortitude.

- **Embracing discomfort:** Change often involves stepping outside of our comfort zones and facing uncertainty. Embracing discomfort as a natural part of the growth process allows individuals to expand their horizons, build resilience, and discover new strengths and capacities within themselves.

- **Cultivating a spirit of curiosity and experimentation:** Embracing change requires a willingness to explore new possibilities, take calculated risks, and experiment with different approaches. By approaching change with a spirit of curiosity and openness, individuals can discover new passions, interests, and opportunities for growth.

Ultimately, embracing change is a courageous act of self-discovery and transformation one that requires openness, adaptability, and a willingness to step into the unknown. By embracing change as a natural part of life's journey, individuals can unlock their full potential and create a life of purpose, fulfillment, and authenticity.

The Power of Mindset

In Embracing Growth this section delves into the transformative power of mindset an internal lens through which we interpret and navigate the world around us.

The section begins by highlighting the profound influence that our thoughts and beliefs have on shaping our reality. Our mindset the collection of beliefs, attitudes, and assumptions that shape our perceptions and behaviors plays a pivotal role in determining our level of success, fulfillment, and overall well-being.

At the heart of mindset is the distinction between a fixed mindset and a growth mindset. Individuals with a fixed mindset believe that their abilities, talents, and intelligence are static traits that cannot be changed. In contrast, those with a growth mindset believe that their abilities can be developed and strengthened through effort, practice, and learning.

Cultivating a growth mindset involves fostering self-belief, resilience, and optimism in the face of challenges and setbacks. It requires recognizing that failure is not a reflection of our inherent worth or abilities but rather an opportunity for growth and learning. By reframing setbacks as valuable learning experiences and embracing a "yet" mentality recognizing that we may not have mastered a skill or achieved a goal "yet" individuals can cultivate a sense of perseverance and resilience in pursuit of their goals.

This section further explores various strategies and practices for cultivating a growth mindset, including:

- **Practicing self-awareness:** Developing awareness of our thoughts, beliefs, and self-talk is the first step toward cultivating a growth mindset. By noticing and challenging negative or limiting beliefs, individuals can begin to reframe their thinking and adopt a more positive and empowering mindset.
- **Embracing challenges:** Viewing challenges as opportunities for growth and learning is a hallmark of a growth mindset. Instead of avoiding difficult tasks or situations, individuals with a growth mindset embrace challenges as opportunities to stretch their abilities, build resilience, and develop new skills.
- **Cultivating resilience:** Resilience is the ability to bounce back from adversity and adapt to changing circumstances. By building resilience through practices such as positive self-talk, social support,

and mindfulness, individuals can navigate life's ups and downs with greater ease and grace.

- **Adopting an optimistic outlook:** Optimism is a key characteristic of a growth mindset. By maintaining a positive outlook and focusing on solutions rather than dwelling on problems, individuals can cultivate a sense of hope, agency, and possibility in their lives.

- **Embracing lifelong learning:** Embracing a growth mindset involves recognizing that learning is a lifelong journey. By seeking out new experiences, challenging themselves to learn new skills, and remaining open to feedback and constructive criticism, individuals can continue to grow and evolve throughout their lives.

Ultimately, cultivating a growth mindset empowers individuals to harness the power of our minds to create the life we desire. By fostering self-belief, resilience, and optimism, individuals can overcome obstacles, achieve their goals, and unlock our full potential for personal and professional growth.

The Journey Continues

Now let us reflect on the ongoing nature of the personal growth journey and the importance of embracing each experience as an opportunity for learning, growth, and evolution.

We need to acknowledge that personal growth is not a destination but rather a continuous journey a journey that unfolds over a lifetime and is marked by a series of experiences, challenges, and opportunities for growth. It emphasizes the importance of adopting a mindset of curiosity, openness, and willingness to learn as we navigate the twists and turns of our individual paths.

Central to this section is the idea that every experience we encounter whether positive or negative, joyful, or challenging has the potential to serve as a catalyst for growth and transformation. By embracing each experience with curiosity and a willingness to learn, we can extract valuable lessons and insights that propel us forward on our journey.

This section encourages you to approach life with a sense of mindfulness and presence, recognizing that growth occurs not only in moments of triumph but also in moments of struggle and uncertainty. It emphasizes the importance of cultivating self-awareness and self-reflection as tools for gaining deeper insights into ourselves and our patterns of behavior.

Furthermore, this section emphasizes the power of resilience the ability to bounce back from adversity and adapt to changing circumstances as a key ingredient in navigating life's ups and downs. It encourages you to view setbacks not as roadblocks but as opportunities for growth and learning, reminding you that you possess the inner strength and resilience to overcome any obstacle that comes their way.

Ultimately, "The Journey Continues" serves as a reminder that personal growth is a lifelong process an ongoing journey of self-exploration, discovery, and transformation. It encourages you to embrace each moment with a sense of curiosity, openness, and optimism, knowing that they hold the power to shape our own destiny and create a life filled with meaning, purpose, and fulfillment.

Overcoming

Overcoming an unhealthy past or present is a courageous step towards embracing growth and creating a more fulfilling life. Here are some strategies to support your journey:

- **Seek therapy:** Professional therapy or counseling can provide a safe and supportive space to explore and heal from past traumas, negative patterns, and emotional wounds. A qualified therapist can offer guidance, tools, and techniques to address underlying issues and promote healing and growth.

- **Practice self-care:** Prioritize self-care activities that nourish your body, mind, and spirit. This may include regular exercise, healthy eating, sufficient sleep, mindfulness practices, relaxation techniques, and engaging in activities that bring you joy and fulfillment.

- **Challenge negative beliefs:** Identify and challenge any negative beliefs or self-limiting beliefs that may be holding you back. Replace these with more empowering and affirming beliefs that support your growth and well-being.
- **Cultivate self-compassion:** Practice self-compassion and kindness towards yourself, especially during challenging times. Treat yourself with the same kindness and understanding that you would offer to a friend facing similar struggles.
- **Set boundaries:** Establish healthy boundaries in your relationships and interactions to protect your well-being and honor your needs and preferences. Learn to say no to activities, obligations, or people that drain your energy or compromise your values.
- **Develop coping skills:** Build a toolkit of coping skills and strategies to manage stress, anxiety, and other difficult emotions effectively. This may include mindfulness practices, deep breathing exercises, journaling, creative expression, or seeking support from trusted friends or family members.
- **Forgive yourself and others:** Practice forgiveness towards yourself and others for past mistakes, hurts, or disappointments. Holding onto resentment or guilt can hinder your ability to move forward and embrace growth. Release the burden of resentment and embrace forgiveness as a path to healing and liberation.

- **Set goals and take action:** Identify specific goals or aspirations that align with your values and vision for the future. Break these goals down into actionable steps and commit to taking consistent, intentional action towards their realization. Celebrate your progress along the way and adjust your course as needed.

- **Stay present:** Practice mindfulness and presence in the moment, focusing on the here and now rather than dwelling on the past or worrying about the future. Cultivate gratitude for the blessings and opportunities in your life, fostering a sense of peace, contentment, and acceptance.

- **Seek support:** Surround yourself with supportive and uplifting individuals who believe in your potential and encourage your growth journey. Lean on friends, family members, support groups, or mentors who can offer guidance, encouragement, and perspective along the way.

Remaining consistent in your growth journey can indeed be challenging, but there are several strategies you can employ to help stay on track:

- **Set Clear Goals:** Clearly define your goals and aspirations, breaking them down into smaller, manageable steps. Having a clear roadmap will provide you with direction and motivation to stay consistent.

- **Create a Routine:** Establishing a regular routine or schedule can help you stay organized and make it easier to incorporate growth-promoting activities into your daily life. Consistency breeds habit, so aim to make positive behaviors a regular part of your routine.
- **Stay Accountable:** Find ways to hold yourself accountable for your actions and commitments. This could involve tracking your progress, setting deadlines, or sharing your goals with a friend, mentor, or coach who can provide support and encouragement.
- **Practice Self-Discipline:** Cultivate self-discipline by learning to prioritize your goals and stay focused on the tasks at hand. This may involve saying no to distractions, delaying gratification, and overcoming procrastination.
- **Celebrate Small Wins:** Acknowledge and celebrate your achievements, no matter how small they may seem. Recognizing your progress and accomplishments can boost your confidence and motivation to keep moving forward.
- **Stay Flexible:** Be willing to adapt and adjust your approach as needed. Life is full of unexpected twists and turns, so it's essential to remain flexible and resilient in the face of challenges or setbacks.
- **Find Inspiration:** Surround yourself with sources of inspiration and motivation that fuel your desire for

growth. This could include reading inspiring books, listening to motivational podcasts, or connecting with like-minded individuals who share your aspirations.

- **Practice Self-Compassion:** Be kind and understanding towards yourself, especially during times when you may struggle to maintain consistency. Acknowledge that setbacks are a natural part of the journey and treat yourself with the same compassion you would offer to a friend facing similar challenges.
- **Visualize Success:** Use visualization techniques to imagine yourself achieving your goals and experiencing the rewards of your efforts. Visualization can help reinforce your commitment and keep your eyes on the prize.
- **Stay Persistent:** Above all, remember that consistency is a long- term commitment, and it's normal to encounter obstacles along the way. Stay persistent, stay focused on your goals, and trust in your ability to overcome challenges and realize your dreams.

Overcoming obstacles and maintaining consistency are essential components of personal growth and development. Here's a detailed explanation of why they are important:

- **Overcoming Obstacles:**

Promotes Resilience: Overcoming challenges builds resilience, which is the ability to bounce back from adversity. Resilience enables individuals to cope with stress, setbacks, and trauma more effectively, fostering mental and emotional strength.

Fosters Growth: Every obstacle presents an opportunity for growth and learning. By overcoming challenges, individuals develop new skills, gain valuable insights, and become more adaptable, leading to personal and professional development.

Builds Confidence: Successfully navigating obstacles boosts self-confidence and self-efficacy the belief in one's ability to achieve goals. Confidence empowers individuals to take on new challenges with courage and optimism, leading to further success.

Strengthens Character: Facing and overcoming adversity helps individuals develop strong character traits such as perseverance, determination, and grit. These qualities are essential for achieving long-term goals and overcoming future obstacles.

- **Being Consistent:**

Creates Habits: Consistency is the key to forming positive habits. By repeatedly engaging in desired behaviors over time, they become ingrained in our daily routine, making them easier to maintain in the long run.

Builds Momentum: Consistent action builds momentum toward our goals. Just as a small snowball grows larger as it rolls downhill, consistent effort compounds over time, leading to significant progress and results.

Ensures Progress: Consistency is crucial for making steady progress toward our goals. Even small, incremental steps taken consistently can lead to significant achievements over time, whereas sporadic effort often yields limited or inconsistent results.

Develops Discipline: Consistency requires discipline and commitment to prioritize long-term goals over short-term gratification. Developing discipline strengthens willpower and self-control, enabling individuals to resist distractions and stay focused on their objectives.

Increases Accountability: Consistent action holds individuals accountable for their goals and commitments. When we consistently show up and put in the effort, we demonstrate our dedication and accountability to ourselves and others, fostering trust and credibility.

In summary, overcoming obstacles and being consistent are essential for personal growth and success. By embracing challenges, learning from setbacks, and staying committed to our goals with unwavering consistency, we can unlock our full potential, achieve meaningful results, and lead fulfilling lives.

Communication is Key

Communication plays a pivotal role in our journey as we are embracing our growth. Here are some reasons why:

- **Self-expression:** Effective communication allows us to express our thoughts, emotions, and experiences, facilitating introspection and self-awareness. By articulating our feelings and desires, we gain clarity about our values, aspirations, and areas for personal development.
- **Connection:** Communication fosters connection and understanding with others, enabling us to build supportive relationships and communities. Through open and honest dialogue, we share our experiences, learn from others, and receive encouragement and feedback that propel us forward on our journey.
- **Conflict resolution:** As we navigate challenges and conflicts on our path to growth, communication serves as a vital tool for resolving differences and fostering reconciliation. By engaging in constructive dialogue, we can address misunderstandings, negotiate solutions, and strengthen our interpersonal connections.
- **Learning and growth:** Communication enables us to exchange ideas, perspectives, and knowledge with others, facilitating continuous learning and personal growth. By engaging in meaningful conversations, seeking feedback, and embracing diverse

viewpoints, we expand our understanding of the world and enrich our own perspectives.

- **Goal setting and accountability:** Effective communication helps us articulate our goals, aspirations, and action plans, enabling us to set clear intentions and hold ourselves accountable for our progress. By sharing our goals with others and seeking their support and accountability, we enhance our motivation and commitment to personal growth.

- **Empowerment:** Communication empowers us to advocate for ourselves, assert our needs and boundaries, and take ownership of our lives. By advocating for our rights and expressing our preferences, we assert agency and autonomy in shaping our journey of growth and transformation.

In essence, communication serves as a cornerstone of our journey towards self- discovery, empowerment, and fulfillment. By embracing open, honest, and compassionate communication with ourselves and others, we create the foundation for meaningful connections, personal growth, and positive change.

Communication is the process of exchanging information, ideas, thoughts, and feelings between individuals or groups through various channels such as verbal, nonverbal, written, or visual cues. It encompasses both sending and receiving messages, and it plays a fundamental role in human interaction and relationships.

Our communication is shaped by a variety of factors, including:

- **Personal experiences:** Your past experiences, interactions, and relationships influence how you communicate with others. Positive experiences may enhance your communication skills and confidence, while negative experiences may lead to communication barriers or challenges.
- **Cultural background:** Your cultural background, including norms, values, beliefs, and traditions, significantly influences your communication style and preferences. Cultural differences in communication can affect how messages are interpreted and understood by individuals from different cultural backgrounds.
- **Social environment:** Your social environment, including family, friends, peers, and colleagues, shapes your communication patterns and behaviors. Observing and interacting with others in social settings can influence your language use, communication styles, and interpersonal dynamics.
- **Personality traits:** Your personality traits, such as extroversion, introversion, assertiveness, empathy, and openness, impact how you express yourself and engage with others in communication. These traits

may influence your communication preferences, tendencies, and effectiveness in different contexts.

- **Education and upbringing:** Your education level, upbringing, and exposure to formal education or training programs may affect your communication skills, vocabulary, grammar, and language proficiency. Formal education can provide you with knowledge and tools to communicate effectively in various settings.

- **Media and technology:** The proliferation of media platforms, digital communication tools, and social media networks has transformed how people communicate and interact with each other. Your exposure to media and technology can influence your communication habits, preferences, and reliance on digital communication channels.

Overall, your communication is shaped by a complex interplay of personal, cultural, social, psychological, and environmental factors. Understanding these factors can help you become more aware of your communication style, adapt to diverse communication contexts, and improve your overall communication effectiveness.

5 Patterns of Communication

Unequal - Unequal communication patterns are identified as blamer, placate, irrelevant, and super-reasonable. These are people who gain strength and self- esteem through the criticism of others. They are the blamer, faultfinder, a dictator, and a boss.

Pleasers – These are people who demeans themselves while at the same time boosting others. Consequently, the pleasing communicator is a "yes person," who always tries to give pleasure to everyone else, constantly apologizes, and never recognizes their own voice or identity.

Isolated - Isolated communicators has a scarcity of self-confidence, and their participation often seems entirely unrelated to the issue currently being addressed.

Tremendously Rational – Tremendously rational communicators as dispassionate and robot-like, always feeling as though they must control both themselves and others involved. Tremendously rational communicators gather muscle from pretending they know it all while simultaneously causing their audience to appear ignorant.

Harmonious - Harmonious communication suggests to communication that displays no incongruence within its own communication. Harmonious communicators "discloses their thoughts and emotions about themselves without casting them onto others and thus escaping manipulation."

- ▶ **Judgment:** Select if your words need to be filtered.
- ▶ **Intention:** Am I saying this to sow seeds of discord and hate or am I seeking a peaceful solution.
- ▶ **Choice:** Does this need to be said.

- ▶ **Compassion:** Can I try to see how the other party feels.
- ▶ **Empathy:** Can I view the other person's point of view.
- ▶ **Evaluation:** Was I problematic or resolution?

Anger is always a secondary emotion cause by a primary emotion such as fear, hurt or frustration. Martin Luther said: "When I am angry, I can write, pray and preach well, for then my whole temperament is quickened, my understanding sharpened, and all mundane vexations and temptations are gone."

In a healthy home people have learned how to listen, ask questions, and nurture quality communication. As goes the communication so goes the relationship.

Without communication, there is no relationship. Of course, this principle applies to all our relationships: parent and child, brother and sister, pastor and congregation, employer, and employee as well as friend and friend.

How can something that seems so simple as talking be so difficult? One reason is that many people don't understand the complexities of clear communication. If you want to increase the quality of your communication here are several simple things to keep in mind.

First, remember that quality communication takes time. Since good communication doesn't just happen, smart families set aside a regular time each week for focused communication.

A second principle is that quality communication involves more than words. Many assume that if we just use the right words others will understand what we mean.

Communication can be difficult because often what we intend to say and what the other person thinks we meant can be substantially different. Actual words we say only account for 7% of how someone interprets our message. Our tone of voice accounts for 38% and other non-verbal's such as body posture, gestures, eye contact and facial expressions account for 55%.

Don't miss this next point! Marriages and families (relationships) are NOT destroyed by differences. They are destroyed by the immature, irresponsible and unhealthy ways we choose to respond to those differences. They are destroyed by our inability or unwillingness to take them to God and allow Him to teach us how to learn and grow from them.

In Romans 15 we are encouraged to "be of the same mind," to "accept one another" and to "admonish one another." This is especially applicable in marriage. Relationships involve people coming together. However, in that process we find that our differences can lead to disagreements that at times result in conflict.

Our differences- when understood, appreciated-can be used of God to help us, in the words of Proverbs, to "sharpen" one another. What do you get when iron rubs against iron? Heat. Sparks fly. But if the pieces are rubbed together in the right way, they inevitably sharpen each other.

1. Conflict is inevitable. An occupational hazard of being human is that if you are in any relationship for any length of time you will experience conflict.
2. Most conflict isn't dealt with in healthy ways because most of us don't know how or have undelivered areas in our life from the past. When faced with conflict we personalize it, interpret it as an attack or to see only one solution . . . ours.
3. Healthy conflict provides opportunities for growth.
4. Unresolved conflicts interfere with growth and satisfying relationships. Problems don't magically disappear. They go underground and grow into other problems. The more you deny, hide from, overlook, and avoid conflict the greater the problem will become. AVOIDANCE IS NOT DELIVERANCE!
5. Conflict isn't good or bad, right, or wrong . . . conflict simply is. It is how we choose to respond to conflict that creates the problem or produces the growth.
6. Constructive conflict involves a commitment to serve, encourage and be vulnerable to one another.
7. Constructive conflict involves a commitment to stop, look, and listen, then, maybe, speak.

We try to show the other person where THEY are wrong, and WE are right. How many times in your life has that helped?

The next time conflict stares you in the face try these three simple steps. First, make your primary goal to understand the other person. Take a few minutes to acknowledge, discuss and define the conflict and then listen. Proverbs 17:27- 28 says that "He who restrains his words has knowledge, and he who has a cool spirit is a person of understanding. Even a fool, when he keeps silent, is considered wise."

Step two is to ask yourself, "What is MY contribution to the problem?" Most of us find it easier to identify the other person's contribution to the problem, how "they" need to change and what "they" could do different, rather than our own.

The third step is to commit yourself to understand what the issue looks like through their eyes. Proverbs 25:12 tells us that, "It is badge of honor to accept valid criticism." Listen to what the other person has to say. Even if you think that 90% of what they're saying isn't valid, listen for the 10% that might be true. Look for even the 1% that God could use in your life to help you deepen and mature.

Proverbs 12:18 tells us that, "The tongue of the wise brings healing."

May this eBook serve as a guiding light on your path towards embracing growth, unlocking your true potential, and living a life filled with meaning, purpose, and fulfillment." This concluding statement in "Embracing Growth: A Journey of Self- Exploration and Transformation" encapsulates the overarching message of the book and serves as a heartfelt wish for your journey ahead.

Please acknowledge the transformative power of the eBook, envisioning it as a beacon of inspiration and guidance for those embarking on their own paths of personal growth and self-discovery. It recognizes that the journey towards embracing growth is not always easy, but it is immensely rewarding and worth pursuing wholeheartedly.

Furthermore, the statement emphasizes your agency and autonomy in shaping your own story. Reminding you that you are the authors of your own lives, with the power to create the narrative you desire. By embracing the journey with an open heart and a courageous spirit, you can navigate life's challenges with resilience, optimism, and grace.

In conclusion, healthy and respectful communication is the cornerstone of positive relationships, effective conflict resolution, and personal growth. By fostering open, honest, and empathetic communication, individuals can build trust, promote understanding, and strengthen connections with others. From resolving conflicts and collaborating effectively to supporting emotional well-being and empowering individuals, the benefits of healthy communication extend to all aspects of life.

As we strive to create a more harmonious and connected world, let us prioritize communication that uplifts, empowers, and fosters mutual respect and understanding. By embracing the principles of healthy and respectful communication, we can cultivate deeper connections, navigate challenges with grace, and build a brighter future for ourselves and those around us.